BLACK CAB WISDOM

Summersdale Publishers Ltd
46 West Street
Chichester
West Sussex
PO19 1RP
UK

www.summersdale.com

Printed and bound in Czech Republic

ISBN: 978 1 84953 126 9

p.116, extract from 'Little Gidding' from *Four Quartets* by T. S. Eliot reproduced by kind permission of Faber and Faber Ltd

Disclaimer
Every effort has been made to attribute the quotations in this collection to the correct source. Should there be any omissions or errors in this respect we apologise and shall be pleased to make the appropriate acknowledgements in any future edition.

Substantial discounts on bulk quantities of Summersdale books are available to corporations, professional associations and other organisations. For details contact Summersdale Publishers by telephone: +44 (0) 1243 771107, fax: +44 (0) 1243 786300 or email: nicky@summersdale.com.

BLACK CAB
WISDOM

Knowledge from the Back Seat

MARK SOLOMON

Introduction

As usual it was just me, myself and I sitting in my London cab. After waiting for what had seemed like an eternity, I finally made it to the front of the taxi rank at Waterloo station. My eyes were fixed on an archway that led potential passengers out from the station concourse. At last! A would-be passenger finally appeared. An elderly gentleman was striding towards my taxi cab: medium height, smartly dressed, well groomed and classy. In a gentle American accent he politely asked me to take him to the Brooks's Club in St James's.

'Jump in, mate,' I replied.

I knew he was worldly wise, I knew he'd been around the block a few times. I just had to ask him.

'Excuse me, sir, what's the best bit of advice you've ever been given?'

He thought for a moment and then said, 'You will have to give me some time to think about that.'

I focused on the journey, and about 25 seconds later…

'Excuse me, driver.'

'Yes?'

'The answer to your question is "Think before you decide".'

'Thanks, mate.'

To his credit, he had practised what he'd preached.

After this auspicious start, I decided to set myself a project: collecting words of 'wisdom' from the passengers that I picked up in my black cab.

I created a gentle pitch to encourage passengers to contribute their favourite quotes and proverbs. From the very beginning, the feedback and contributions were phenomenal. My passengers clearly felt they were part of something special, and the advice I was receiving was without doubt having a positive effect on me. It wasn't long before the success of each working shift was summed up by the number of quotes I had collected, rather than the fares!

The contributors came from all age groups, races, nationalities and religions. Their occupations included a United States senator, a gangster rapper, bankers, tradesmen and even a dolphin trainer. The one thing they all had in common was the fact that they'd journeyed in the back of my London taxi.

Words cannot really convey how grateful I am to the thousands of amazing passengers who kindly shared their words of wisdom with me. After all, they had hired space in the back of my cab and owed me nothing but the fare. Perhaps the most appropriate way to thank all of those passengers, and the team at Summersdale Publishers, is by means of a phrase, and that is…

'You've really started something here!'

Mark Solomon

Just because you're paranoid, it doesn't mean that they're not out to get you.

Paul, Scotland
(Colin Sautar)

Everyone has a photographic memory; it's just that some don't have film.

Cybil, production
(Steven Wright)

The grass may be greener on the other side, but it's just as hard to mow.

Sharron, solicitor

If you're not listening to life, it will remind you.

Steve K, consultant and training mentor

Don't cry because it's over, smile because it happened.

Peter, court clerk
(Dr Seuss)

Positive things come to positive people.

Naomi Cleaver, designer and author

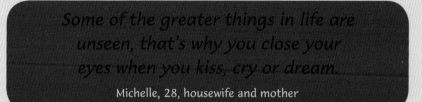

Some of the greater things in life are unseen, that's why you close your eyes when you kiss, cry or dream.

Michelle, 28, housewife and mother

If you don't like the dark side
of the moon, stay in the sun.

Stephen, judge

A man is free the moment
he believes he is.

Alex, urban design student
(Voltaire)

If you think your life is
bland, then you haven't
added enough flavour.

Donna, MBA student

When you are green you are growing!
When you are red you are ripe!
When you are ripe you rot.

Paul, sportsman

Life is not defined by the number of breaths we take, but by the number of moments that take our breath away!

Lauren, Burnley

It's not what happens to you in life, but how you deal with it.

Emily, 30, unemployed

Anyone who has never made a mistake has never tried anything new.

Adnan
(Albert Einstein)

You only appreciate the magnificence of the highest mountain if you've been to the deepest valley.

Steve and partner, Wales
(Richard Nixon)

Every man dies.
Not every man really lives.

Stephanie, aesthetics manager, Hackney
(William Wallace)

What would you do today if you woke up tomorrow and it was 50 years later?

Puja, sustainability investor

What would you do if you knew you couldn't fail?

Andrew, 41, unemployed

If a life is worth living, it's worth living once.
Don't take the risk and just exist.

Lizzie, deputy head teacher

Be daring, be different.

Al

(Cecil Beaton)

The aim of life is to live a
bit more fully each day.

Nathaniel, 29, chef

Two choices today: take it or leave it!

Kay R, Channel Islands

Don't mistake existing for living.

Helena, PR

There's a whole world out there, it's a shame to keep making up excuses to avoid experiencing it.

Jim D

We applaud extraordinary people who live extraordinary lives, but the real praise should go to those who make the ordinary extraordinary.

James, 34, lawyer

Live life to the full, but don't take advantage of its fruits.

Curtis, art student

Some people have a hearth burning in their soul, and yet no one comes to warm themselves by it.

Justin Lee Collins, television and radio presenter
(Vincent van Gogh)

Life will give you thousands of reasons to cry, but show the world that you have millions of reasons to smile.

Joan, Saudi Arabia

To finish first, first you have to finish.

Peter
(Ron Dennis)

You do not have to be great to get started, but you have to start off to be great.

Minesh, Mumbai, India

Between saying and doing, there is a sea.

Dario

Small minds discuss people, average minds discuss events, great minds don't discuss, they do.

Dan, Eton student

Live as if you were going to die tomorrow. Learn as if you will live forever.

Ian, South Africa
(Gandhi)

First do what is necessary, then what is possible,
and then make the impossible possible.

JB, London
(St Francis of Assisi)

Add 'ry' to 'can't'
and you'll get 'can try'.

Jadie-Rose

Whatever you can do, or dream you can do, begin it. Boldness has genius, power and magic in it.

Angie
(Johann Wolfgang von Goethe)

> *Make every decision as if you know it to be right.*
>
> David, company director

> You are not only responsible for the things you do; you are also responsible for the things you don't do.
>
> Michael, 27, air traffic controller, Switzerland

> A moment of action is worth more than a year of thought.
>
> Simon

It's not about whether the wind blows; it's about how you position your sails.

Harry H, entrepreneur

Smooth seas do not make skilful sailors.

BB, Mongolia
(African proverb)

If you want to discover new oceans, you have to be brave enough to lose sight of the shore.

Roger F
(André Gide)

There are those in life who have tried and failed, and those who have never tried at all.

PR, feminist academic

Do what you can, can what you can't.

Donna, student

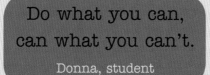

You miss 100 per cent of the shots you don't take.

Rossa Shanks, 27 (Wayne Gretzky)

There are those of us who stop to ask 'why',
and those who dream and ask 'why not?'

James, consultant, Manchester

Keep your eyes on the stars,
and your feet on the ground.

Anonymous
(Theodore Roosevelt)

The best way to make
your dreams come
true is to wake up.

Anonymous
(Paul Valéry)

Life is like a set of stairs, if you look back you will trip up.

Bonnia, online media

Look after your body. It's the only place you've got to live.

Kelly, dietician

However appealing it feels, never go back on life's journey; it's rarely the same and often leads to disappointment.

Jon

In life, big things become small, and small things become big.

Joe, property finance
(Heraclitus)

Always, always, always, keep a steady nerve and take your time.

Sebastian, surgeon

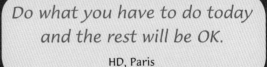

You deserve what you tolerate.

Ronn, entertainment executive, USA

Do what you have to do today
and the rest will be OK.

HD, Paris

A little, often.

Sim, London

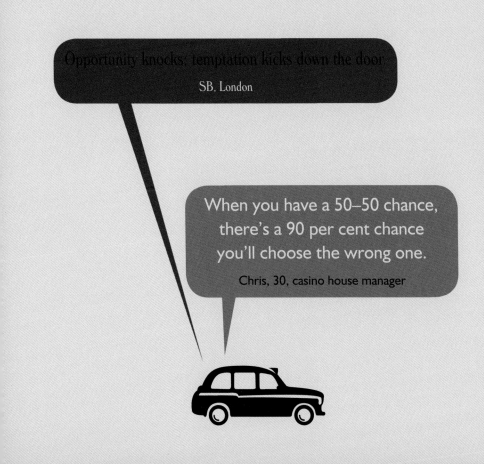

Even if you are on the right track,
if you stop, you get run over!

Marc
(Will Rogers)

Some decisions are best made with the head and some with the heart. The key to success in life is knowing which one to choose.

Anthony, 30, dolphin trainer

Stand before it and there is no beginning. Follow it and there is no end.

Chukka, martial artist
(Lao Tzu)

On the whole, I've found that you're not taken seriously until you're older and uglier!

Mrs Jones, fashion designer

It's not the years in your life that count, but the life in your years.

Vivien, medical secretary
(Abraham Lincoln)

All foxes grow old,
not all grow grey.

Ross B

Don't be scared of the dead.
Be scared of the living.

John, former Grenadier Guard, coal miner and brewery worker

The challenge ahead is never greater than the power behind us.

Charlie W, team leader

Respect the things you did do, not the things you didn't do.

Karen, policewoman

Far better is it to dare mighty things, to win glorious triumphs, even though checkered by failure... than to rank with those poor spirits who neither enjoy much nor suffer much, because they live in a grey twilight that knows not victory nor defeat.

Elizabeth Tan, actress
(Theodore Roosevelt)

*It's not the fear of the thing itself,
but the fear you bring to it.*

Amanda, 46, marketing director
(Marcus Aurelius)

Fall seven times, stand up eight.

Faisal and Abdulaziz Abdullah, Saudi Arabia
(Japanese proverb)

A life lived in fear
is a life half lived.

Rachel, business development
(Spanish proverb)

The only limits you have are those you impose.

Helena, Finland

If there's one thing more powerful than a positive attitude, it's a lack of it.

Anonymous

Whatever you do, big or small, do it right or don't do it at all.

Anthony Law

From strength learn gentleness, through gentleness strength will prevail.

Phil, customer care operative

You can choose your actions, but can't always choose the consequences.

Teisha, lawyer

Be brilliant. If you can't be brilliant, be useful.

Elspeth Lynn, creative director

Courage is not having the energy to go on.
It's going on when you don't have the energy.

Peter, surveyor
(Dame Ellen MacArthur)

To do a mundane task with style is preferable to doing a dangerous one without any.

Amy, Los Angeles, USA

Always try to get to the top of the ladder, just make sure the ladder is leaning against the right wall.

Sapna and Gurj

Why should anyone be led by you?

John, 53, accountant

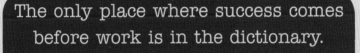

The only place where success comes before work is in the dictionary.

ADB, London
(Vince Lombardi)

Hire people bigger than you and you will create a company of giants.

Barry, advertising
(David Ogilvy)

It's not a free country, everything is bought and sold and owned.

Trevor, publishing
(Charles Bukowski)

Paralysis by analysis.
Don't overanalyse things.

Grant, banking, Australia

The road to success is always under construction.

AF, Norway
(Lily Tomlin)

The road to success is filled with many tempting parking spaces.

Mark Jones, CEO

Success does not make you happy, but happiness makes you successful.

Anita, doctor

Set the bar twice as high as you ever think you can achieve, then if you only go half way you would have achieved a great deal!

David Haye, boxer, former WBA World Heavyweight Champion

Cream always rises to the top, but it also goes off.

Paul, 35

Ability may get you to the top but it takes character to keep you there.

Steve
(John Wooden)

Your next breath is more valuable than your next quid.

Chen, travel agent

A good man in an evil society seems to be the greatest villain of all.

Lionel, UK

If you win the rat race, you're still a rat.

Richard

(Lily Tomlin)

No good deed goes unpunished.

Barry R

The four rules of politics: 1. Keep the initiative;
2. Exploit the inevitable; 3. Stay in with outs;
4. Never stand between a dog and a lamppost.

Anonymous

In politics your opponents are in the other party,
your enemies are in your own party.

Diane Abbott MP

Never doubt the ability of a
small committed group of
people to change the world.

Jon, mining
(Margaret Mead)

If I can see further than anyone else, it is only because I am standing on the shoulders of giants.

Rob, advertising
(Isaac Newton)

We can't always build the future for our youth, but we can build our youth for the future.

Catherine, theatre
(Franklin D. Roosevelt)

People blame our generation, but have they thought of who raised us?

Emily, 14, Norway

A man is the head of the family, but the woman is the neck.

Nat, Becky and Jo
(Chinese proverb)

One wife, one friend. Two wives, two enemies.

Ahmed K, Saudi Arabia

A man is what he thinks about all day long.

Greg, insolvency practitioner
(Ralph Waldo Emerson)

We may not have it all together,
but together we have it all.

Steve and Maria

A minute of perfection was worth the effort. A moment was the most you could ever expect from perfection.

Chuck Palahniuk, novelist and journalist

People are thirstier for love
than they are for water.

Ausra, Lithuania

The one who gets lost in his
passion loses less than the one
who has lost his passion.

Rachel H, Shepherd's Bush

Love knows not its own depth
until the hour of separation.

Matthew
(Khalil Gibran)

To the world you may be just one person,
to one person you may be the world.

Charlotte, advertising
(Brandi Snyder)

A true friend is one who knows
the song in your heart, and
can sing it back to you when
you've forgotten the words.

David

One true friend is better than
a thousand acquaintances.

Hanna, showroom manager

There are good ships and wood ships, and ships that sail the sea, but the best ships are friendships, and may they always be.

Rosie and Nick, sailors, Westminster
(Old Irish saying)

If you fish at night, you have to dry your nets in the morning.

Dan, finance

In a year from now, people won't necessarily remember what you did together, but they'll definitely remember how you made them feel.

Nir, Israel

Before borrowing money off a friend, decide which one you need most.

Canal, 37, teacher
(American proverb)

Tell me who your friends are, and I'll tell you who you are.

Didem, Turkey

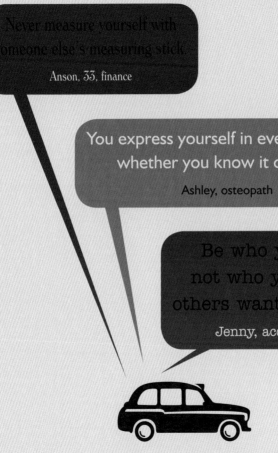

Be a first-rate version of yourself. Not a second-rate version of someone else.

Dan, 36, writer
(Judy Garland)

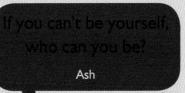

You will be good at something; you just have to find it.

Dave, 44, plumber

If you can't be yourself, who can you be?

Ash

Take half an hour a day to listen to yourself.

Natasha, 18, student

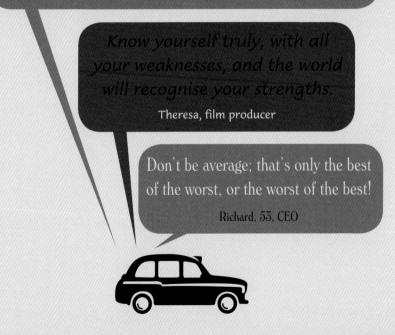

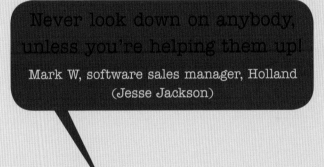

Never look down on anybody,
unless you're helping them up!

Mark W, software sales manager, Holland
(Jesse Jackson)

Never believe that you can deceive.

Wendy, secretary

Set a guard before your mouth;
keep watch at the door of my lips.

Rachel, Australia
(Psalms 141:3)

A smile costs nothing and
yet it enriches so many.

Samantha, head of sustainable developments

We have two ears and one mouth.
Let's use them in that proportion.

Arthur, organic gardener

Waste no time wondering what a good man should be; be one.

Julia, conveyancer
(Marcus Aurelius)

It's not the person underneath,
but your actions that define you.

Dan, concierge

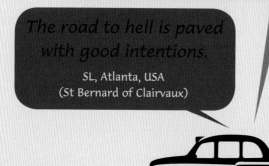

When you point the finger of blame, just remember where the others are pointing.

Graham, roofer

Let people be judged on their worth, rather than their worthlessness.

Anonymous

Attitudes are contagious; is yours worth catching?

Roger, IT service delivery manager

In the mouth of a liar
the truth is doubtful.

Sara, Colombia and Raúl, Cuba and Mexico
(Spanish proverb)

Try looking for the good in people and you'll be amazed what you can find.

Andy, banking

Be kind to strangers because sometimes you're a stranger yourself.

Dave, 36, East London

Be so busy with the improvement of yourself
that you have no time to criticise others.

Amy, actress
(Thomas Jefferson)

It's not what you know, it's who you know, and from who you know, you find out what you know.

Caroline, online media

When people say 'I'm not', they usually are.

Boni Jane, singer

No one can disrespect you without your permission.

Ekow Y, law professor, New York, USA

Not everyone who gets you out of trouble wants to do you good, and not everyone who gets you into trouble wants to do you bad.

Anonymous, Romania

Loose lips sink ships.

Russell B, South London
(English proverb)

Only speak if you'll improve the silence.

Keith and Priscilla, New York City, USA

Always be prepared to understand other people's perspective.

The Panda

Is it kind, is it true, is it necessary?

Poppy, 28, architect
(Sri Sathya Sai Baba)

Don't raise your voice, improve your argument.

Abdul, 26, student, Qatar
(Desmond Tutu)

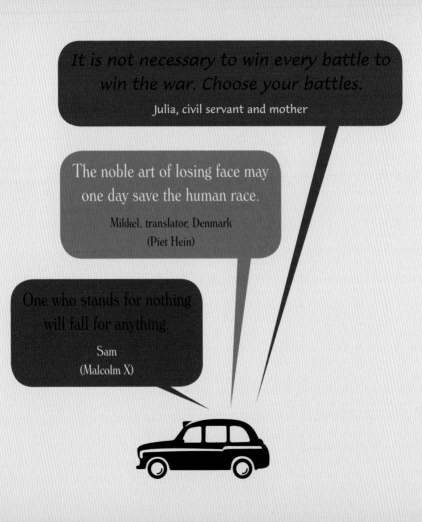

Holding on to anger is like grasping a hot coal with the intent of throwing it at someone else. At the end of the day, you are the one who gets burned.

Vok, Belgrade
(Buddha)

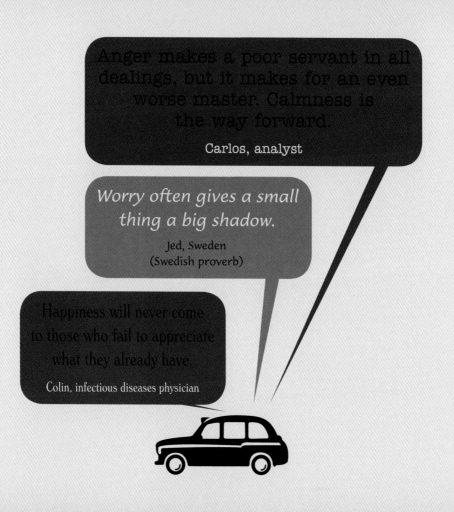

If a voice inside your head says 'You cannot paint', by all means paint, and then the voice will be silent.

Catherine, Melbourne, Australia
(Vincent van Gogh)

Happiness writes white. It does not show up on the page.

Claudia Hammond, presenter of
All in the Mind, BBC Radio 4
(Henri de Montherlant)

Words are the most powerful drug used by mankind.

David, editor
(Rudyard Kipling)

A paragraph should be like a lady's skirt: long enough to cover the essentials but short enough to keep it interesting.

Claire, travel agent

The first rule of writing is applying the seat of the pants to the chair.

Jakob, writer
(Ernest Hemingway)

An hour in the company of a wise man is worth a thousand pages of a book.

Anonymous

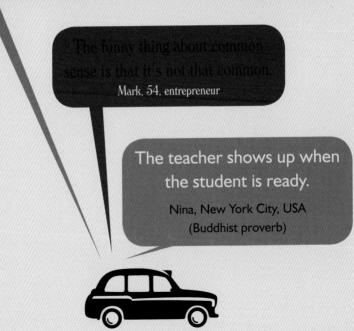

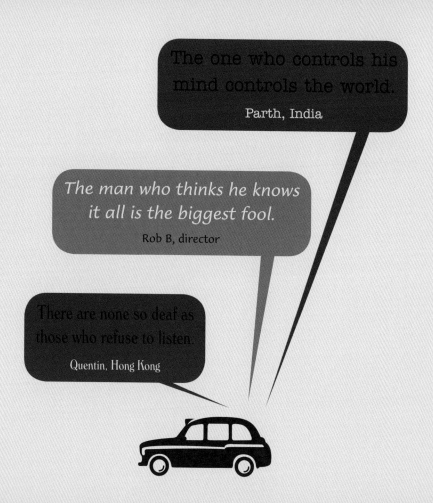

We are what we repeatedly do.
Excellence then, is not an act, but a habit.

Catherine, Melbourne, Australia
(Aristotle)

No brain, no pain.

Ralf, Germany

There is nothing as powerful as an idea whose time has come.

Mark, lawyer
(Victor Hugo)

The entire world is crazy except for me and thee, and sometimes I worry about thee.

Bee, USA

Do one-legged ducks swim in circles? (My response to people who ask me a silly question.)

Mooncat

The definition of madness is doing the same things and expecting a different outcome.

Mike, 33, consultant
(Albert Einstein)

Of all the things I've lost in my life,
I miss my mind the most.

Jane, NHS manager
(Mark Twain)

Embrace the randomness in life.

Filwa, 37, Saudi Arabia

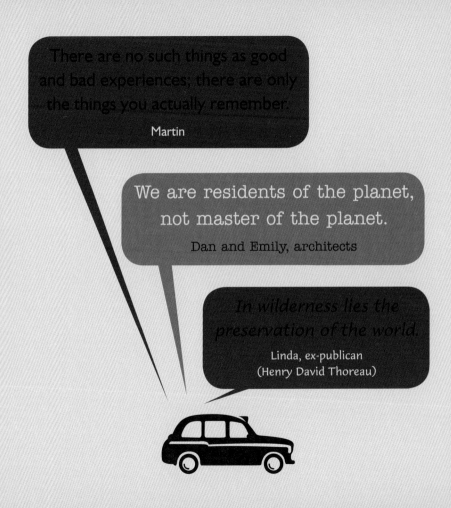

A successful journey begins with a clear sense of destination and a concise plan for achieving it.

Joe, Mexico

If you want to go fast, go alone. If you want to go far, go with friends.

Louise, chef
(African proverb)

> *We shall not cease to explore, and the end of all our exploring will be to return to where we started and know the place for the first time.*
>
> Professor Brian Cox, physicist
> (T. S. Eliot)

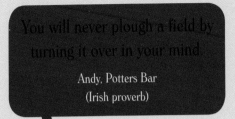

You will never plough a field by turning it over in your mind.

Andy, Potters Bar
(Irish proverb)

The only way to get to the end of the journey is to travel the road that leads to it.

Georgia, 22, Essex

An inch in the right direction is better than a mile in the wrong direction.

Ed, London

A journey of a thousand miles starts with a single step; take one.

Barry, advertising (Confucius)

'What ifs' don't go anywhere.

Richard J, London

The future depends on you!

Victoria, 26, economist, and
Natalia, 22, biologist, Russia

We must use time as a
tool, not as a couch.

Rona
(John F. Kennedy)

Never forget that the passage
of time accelerates as
the deadline approaches.

Julian, politician

There is no future in the past.

Sydney, 28, design engineer

Timing is everything.

Richard, Marlow

Tomorrow doesn't have to
be another yesterday.

Enrico Maria, Italy

Yesterday is history, tomorrow's a mystery, today's a gift, that why it's called the present.

Nourah, 10, Saudi Arabia
(Eleanor Roosevelt)

What is wealth?
Time, children and the
company of friends.

Dermot, Wapping

Everything takes longer than you think. Everything costs more than you think. Nothing is ever finished.

Tony, publisher (His three rules in life.)

Time is the most precious thing you will have; you don't know how much you've got.

Gavin, 39, accountant

History is the migrant parent of the modern world.

Malinda, 25

I hope the best of your past
is the worst of your future!

Harry and Kipper

About the Author

Since becoming a taxi driver back in 1999, Mark Solomon has discovered an eye for photography, a joy in creative writing and a passion for travel. He is a regular contributor to the popular taxi trade newspaper *TAXI*.

In September 2009, Mark began www.blackcabquotes.com, an original and ongoing blog about his collection of words of wisdom from his passengers.

Black Cab Wisdom is Mark's first book. He can still be found driving his iconic London taxi around the city streets, where he continues to gather quotations and proverbs from his passengers.

www.blackcabquotes.com

www.summersdale.com